Y0-BCV-702

COLORADO AND THE ROCKIES

Land of many dreams

First English edition published by Colour Library Books.

99 Park Avenue, New York, N.Y. 10016, U.S.A.
This edition is published by Crescent Books
Distributed by Crown Publishers, Inc.
Display and text filmsetting by Acesetters Ltd., Richmond, Surrey, England.
Printed and bound in Barcelona, Spain.
ISBN 0-517-405512

Crescent 1985.

COLORADO AND THE ROCKIES

Land of many dreams

Text by Bill Harris

Produced by
TED SMART and DAVID GIBBON

CRESCENT BOOKS

The first Europeans found their way to the Rocky Mountains chasing a dream. It was a dream, that is, if you can consider greed and lust a proper inspiration for such things. And in this case the dream was inspired by a pack of lies.

Those first explorers were Spanish. They had long since colonized Mexico and were looking for new riches and adventure. They had brought the Word of God and "civilization," not to mention horses, to the Indians of the Southwest. They had introduced them to slavery, with the natives filling the role of slaves, and they had infected them with diseases the Red Man never knew existed.

By the time they began to move north and established a number of settlements along the Rio Grande down in Texas, word had spread among the Indians that it wasn't all that wonderful to have these people as neighbors. There were two ways to get rid of them. One was to fight, which their brothers to the south had found was a foolish idea, the other was to give them what they seemed to want: new worlds to conquer, preferably rich worlds.

And so the stories began. There are seven great cities to the north, they said. And mountains filled with gold and silver. "Why stay here where all we have are poor farms?" asked the Indians, "when there is so much of what you're looking for just a few day's journey away?" "Why, indeed," replied the Spaniards. And in 1540, Francisco Vasquez de Coronado with an entourage of 400 smartly-outfitted conquistadores, a thousand Indians to take care of them, another thousand horses and mules to carry their gear, herds of goats and sheep to feed them and a procession of priests and monks to make it all seem legitimate, began marching in search of the fabulous Seven Cities of Cibolla.

There are historians who say Coronado never actually set foot in Colorado. Others contend he saw the Royal Gorge. But the story that's the most fun to believe is that the procession crossed paths with a lone Indian who volunteered to show them the way to one of the cities, which he called Quivera, where they would find streets paved with gold and marble houses with precious stones used for windows. For some reason, the Spaniards trusted this particular Indian. Maybe it was because they liked his looks. He looked so much like a Turk they called him "El Turko." Most likely they believed him because they had been trekking over rough terrain for more than a year and hadn't found so much as a zircon.

Whatever the reason, El Turko became Coronado's right-hand man and the hand was pointed north. As they passed from village to village, the Indians, possibly responding to an El Turko wink, would always say, "Oh, yes! You're almost there. Keep on trekking." Somehow, none of those conquistadores, none of those priests, none of those monks, even the great Coronado himself, ever asked: "How come if all those riches are just over the next hill you people aren't living any better than *this*?"

A dream can do that to a man.

El Turko led the parade out to the Great Plains and still they kept going north and east. Finally, after long weeks in the hot sun, it dawned on Coronado that he just might be in the company of a liar. With very little ceremony, he strangled the Indian.

But what if El Turko hadn't been a liar? Coronado couldn't help wondering about that. He set up a winter camp and began making plans to continue his search in the spring.

Meanwhile, one of the time-killing entertainments in the winter camp was horse racing and Coronado was an avid participant. It isn't known whether there were any two-peso bets riding with him, but one of his races ended abruptly when the leader fell from his horse and was trampled by another. The thought of recovering out there in the middle of Kansas dimmed the dream considerably and he ordered his men to strike camp and head back to the Southwest. He never returned.

The Coronado expedition went home no richer than when it had started. But the Spanish Court was convinced that they had just made a wrong turn somewhere and that there were incredible riches in those mountains.

One of the favorites of the Court was a man named Hernan de Soto who had gone to Peru some years before and had taken a treasure away from another Spaniard, Francisco Pizzaro, who had gotten the treasure in the first place by conquering the Incas. De Soto was anxious to find a treasure of his own and got permission to finance an expedition more than twice the size of Coronado's.

His route was up the Mississippi River where his troops had a high old time killing Indians, raping their women and burning their villages. He too wound up in Kansas. While he was there he came down with a fever and died. His troops marched on without him and in 1542 finally made it to the mountains of Colorado. They spent the summer looking for the gold, but when the winter winds started to blow they lost their enthusiasm and, like Coronado, headed for home.

Dreams die hard, though, and for another 250 years, Spanish explorers came and went. Some of them found gold, others found silver. The Indians may have exaggerated, but they weren't lying when they said there were riches in the Rockies.

The French were exploring the Rockies by the early part of the 18th century, but unlike the Spanish who lusted after glory as much as gold and therefor talked a lot, the French believed that the fewer people who knew you were getting rich, the fewer would want to share the wealth. They quietly went about their business, usually alone, and many did, indeed, get rich by hunting and trapping.

There have always been riches for the taking in the Rocky Mountains. But for many, the real riches are the mountains themselves.

The Rocky Mountains are easily the most scenic place in the world, with a naturally rugged and pristine quality that gives different inspiration to different people. The mountains inspire the imagination with visions of indescribable grandeur in many places, visions of complete tranquility in others. Nothing is quite as soul-soothing as listening to the breeze in the trees while you're looking at a peaceful mountain lake in the early evening quiet. No matter where your eye takes you: up at prodigious peaks that are thick with snow-dusted pines in winter; out over wheat fields at midday when light and shadows create a landscape that can only be described as surreal; or through the newly-constructed labyrinth of skyscrapers that compete for attention with the mountains on the horizon in Denver, one of the fastest-growing cities in America, you know that these places, these mountains, are very special places indeed.

The mountains themselves have been here for millions of years and seem determined to remain for millions more in spite of the fact that man has tried over and over again to conquer them, to tame them. No matter what man does, though, he usually ends up coming to terms with their uncompromising force. All who try to change the landscape find out sooner or later that it's best to succumb to its authoritative voice and learn to be obedient to its dominance.

The voice of the mountains is subtle and often undecipherable but it is a voice that one must listen to very carefully. The sound of the wind in the trees can be a signal to a climber that a thunderstorm is coming and a climber who listens well will live to climb again. But people who resist the message will find that tragedy can occur unexpectedly. The mountains will go on living no matter what they do!

The very first explorers found the mountains a barrier. Only the hardiest tried to go through them or over them and it wasn't until the 1850s that the lure of gold made the Rockies a destination for people on the move. Today, of course, Colorado and the Rockies are destinations for travellers from all over the world. Magnificent scenery is one reason. Water is another. The sun is perhaps the most important of all.

The mountains give you a feeling of completion and a sense of renewal all at the same time. They create delight as well as opportunity, a religious reverence as well as a feeling of freedom from the problems of everyday life. A visitor who can feel a process of interaction with nature, an awareness of her controlling influence along with a sensitivity to her vulnerability holds the key to what this landscape has to offer.

The tantalizing beauty of the place overwhelms first-time visitors as well as the people who have spent a lifetime here. But it is a fragile beauty. It must be protected.

A single lifetime isn't enough to take all the pleasure the mountains have to give. But there is another type of taking. On the one hand there are greedy people who seem determined to undermine every attempt by environmentalists to preserve the wild beauty of the West. On the other there are those who understand that being in the mountains is a privilege.

Fortunately, the majority of the people who live here are in the latter group. It's one of the reasons why they live here. The common thread that binds them together is a good-natured attitude. Good-natured in every sense of the word. The understanding that nature is important makes the thread resilient to pressure and opposition and it is an incredibly strong thread. It has made the people capable of fighting for what they believe.

Fortunately, the massive migration to the West in recent years has been joined by people who want to retain the gifts of nature. By and large, the newcomers bring an empathy for the land and all the creatures inhabiting it and the battle against those who don't have such feelings has become easier. But it's a battle our grandchildren will have to fight as well. Not only are there riches under the ground that will always lure the greedy, but there are insensitive, uncaring people who can damage the landscape simply out of sheer ignorance.

Forest fires are possibly the greatest of all things that menace the environment of the Rockies. Ironically, the factor that raises the danger is the very thing that makes the mountains such a perfect vacationland: Colorado has about 300 days of golden sunshine a year. The result is that humidity levels are low and the forests are extremely dry for much of the time.

But if the bright sun plays a part in endangering the wilderness, it also adds to the enjoyment for modern man. When the Indians were the only people here, the sun inspired awe and the Utes believed that it could give a man supernatural powers. The Sun Dance, which their descendants still perform for visitors at the only Indian reservation in Colorado, in the Southwestern corner of the state, was an annual event for men who wanted to gain some of those powers.

The Sun Dance was a five-day event held in mid-July when the sun was considered to be most powerful. The braves, who were not allowed to eat or drink for the duration of the ceremony, gathered in a circular pen that was made of tree branches. In the middle a tall pole topped with a bundle of branches was the focal point of the ceremony and no dancer ever took his eyes off it. Each dancer was given a space along the outer wall with an individual path leading toward the pole in the center and each spent the five days alternately moving backward and forward along his designated path. When they got to the pole, they stayed there for a few minutes gesturing and chanting and communicating with the sun. Usually on the trip back and forth they announced their presence by chanting and blowing whistles made of eagle bones. At some point during the ceremony, whether from hunger, from fatigue or from some sort of self-intoxication, the brave would eventually fall down in a faint. When that happened it was said that they had accumulated all of the sun's power they were capable of absorbing. Naturally the last one to swoon was considered the most powerful.

Modern man draws power from the sun and the Rocky Mountain setting in quite a different way. There is no need to chant, no reason to blow a whistle made of eagle bones. Nothing more is required of you than to stand quietly and look around. What could be more profound than a fresh snowfall, the intricately woven web of a spider, a newborn colt or the natural color of a wildflower? The ambiance of the Rockies is nothing less than exquisite and filled with wonders enough for a lifetime of contemplation.

But there are more people than ever before sharing the experience and the effect of that sometimes upsets the natural balance of the ecosystem and results in an exploitation of the integrity of the land. The mountains that for generations were just a far-off image of splendor for most Americans are now an easy reality for the majority. It is more important than ever to preserve them, before the encroachment of development destroys what nature has given us.

An awareness of the idyllic and untainted beauty of the mountains has become a trademark of a true Westerner. People who live here are as proud of this clean, unexploited environment as were the Indians who worshipped it. Instead of attempting to conquer it, the Indians chose to make friends with it and to become as one with the Almighty God who created it for them. The White Man forced the Indians further west beyond the mountains, considering such a wonderful place too good for so-called savages. Now new arrivals are causing alarm about overcrowding.

Expulsion of the Indians from their mountain home was to be incredibly easy. Though they knew very well how to fight, and often did, they were a passive and peaceful people. They lived a life of serenity, in harmony with nature, which the early settlers took advantage of, but which modern Coloradoans are adopting more and more as their own attitude. With a little luck and plenty of care, this time the story will have a different ending.

The mountains rewarded the Indians with rich clay for their pottery, abundant wildlife for their food and that ever-present sun for their inspiration.

The sun shines through five of every six days, splashing the landscape with a brilliant yellow color that rivals anything any artist could paint. It is a net that holds you and keeps you from ever escaping the lure of the Rockies.

In fact, it is only because the mountains are so enticing and the sunshine so inviting that Westerners succumb to the call that holds them here. The majesty of nature makes you aware of the brevity of life; it causes you to reflect on your priorities and to act on immediate impulses. At the core of the Western spirit is a state of mind that allows you to appreciate the moment and the special freedom it grants you. Westerners feel a need to see and do everything quickly and at the same time to absorb the aesthetics that nature has so generously and elaborately bestowed on them. The options are so diverse, so versatile, so numerous, that Coloradoans expend most of their energy outdoors enjoying the open spaces and the scenic plethora of puzzling delights that give compelling reasons to meditate on the underlying meaning of the Universe. It is a normal human undertaking, but in Colorado it is more intense than almost anywhere else. Our minds can wonder, our bodies can rejoice and our senses celebrate. The beauty of the West is that intense.

The Indians often referred to the Rockies as their "Shining Mountains." The Spaniards were impressed by another quality and named the place "Colorado," actually because of the Colorado River whose waters have a red color that makes it memorable. As they explored it, though, they discovered that the countryside itself abounded in other beautiful colors, vibrant and explosive colors that still dazzle the eye.

The color of the land is an exquisite blend of natural tones ranging from sage green to rust and the deep color of clay. The textures, too, are varied and the variety of geological wonders includes mountains composed entirely of red iron, plateaux thick with clay sediment, deep, dark canyons and majestic rocks that lure climbers of every stripe.

The power that the place held for the early conquistadores still exists as people continue to be mesmerized, by the infinite beauty that is unique to this part of the world.

And why not? It is, as they say, "a picture no artist could paint." How could anything be more emphatic, yet more difficult to recreate on canvas, than a full harvest moon rising over a snow-covered field? Only God could produce a more pleasing combination of colors than can be seen in a purple and violet columbine blowing in the warm breeze wafting across an alpine meadow. And what could be more symbolic of the bounty of nature than a fat, orange pumpkin in a windswept wheat field?

Certainly there can be only one answer: Nature above all is an inexplicable phenomenon. The mountains and what happens within them are an enduring symbol of the cyclical movement of life.

The sounds of life are there, too. A blue jay singing on a lofty pine, the distant howl of a coyote reverberating off a canyon wall, the simple sound of the wind blowing through the trees in the high mountains make us all want to silence our own voices and listen to this great force, the secret language of nature whispering delicately at times, roaring fiercely at other times.

It is clearly the place to be for nature lovers and sports enthusiasts alike. The infinitely optimistic soul willing to bare heart and mind to the elements, which often seem hostile, but always compensate for the struggle with lavish rewards, understands very well what winning is all about. There is no place on earth that can boast the combination of the good, soul-satisfying aspects of life in Colorado and the Rockies.

There is urbanity here, too, in great cities like Denver and the other communities that line Colorado's Front Range, but the good natural life is always at hand. The air is envigorating and gives people a feeling of good health. The mountain slopes that provide the best skiing in the United States in the winter months are transformed in summer to islands of milk and honey because of the melted snow that cascades down the hillsides to the delight of hikers and climbers. Of course, in the high mountain country the snow rarely melts and summer, by the standards of many, never comes.

In the days of the great gold fever in the middle of the last century a lot of men became the first to explore some of those high places. Those who stayed behind were as curious about the climate as they were about the opportunity to get rich. When an old prospector stumbled into Denver in the fall of 1861, the first question he was asked was about the summer temperatures up there. "I don't know what summer's like in the mountains," he said, "I wasn't there but 18 months."

A man could get lost up there; even today in spite of marked trails, paved roads and helpful neighbors.

Colorado is big. At 104,247 square miles, it is the eighth largest state. Its population of 2,889,735 ranks it 28th among the 50 United States. Its borders make drawing maps of it child's play. It is a perfect rectangle with its east-west border extending for 400 miles, the north-south line for 300 miles.

And though Colorado is mountainous, a good deal of the state is composed of level plains and valleys extending some 200 miles west from the prairies to the foothills of the Rockies where, in a band not more than 35 miles wide, about two-thirds of all the people live. Beyond the foothills, 51 mountain peaks more than 14,000 feet high are part of the landscape. The most visible from a distance is Pike's Peak, a piker compared to some (it ranks 28th among Colorado's mountains) because it is only 14,110 feet high. It is so dramatic because it rises straight up without any other surrounding high mountains. When Zebulon Pike, the man who is credited with discovering it, first saw it, he wasn't sure it was a mountain at all, but said in his journal that he had seen a mysterious blue cloud on the horizon.

Fifteen hundred of Colorado's mountains are more than 10,000 feet high, which makes it the highest of all states, including Alaska. Its mean altitude is 6,800 feet, over 1,500 feet more than a mile above sea level. The highest point is Mount Elbert, 14,431 feet, which is not far from the lowest point in the state at Holly, near the Kansas border, where the elevation is 3,385 feet. The vertical difference between the two spots is well over two miles.

People are fond of calling Colorado "the Switzerland of America," and, indeed, there are colonies of Swiss-Americans who have come here because of the comfort of familiarity. But the name was probably dreamed up by the Swiss Tourist Office. The fact is, Colorado has six times the mountain area of Switzerland and the fabled Matterhorn is only 250 feet higher than Mount Elbert.

Just as Colorado is more than the Rockies, the Rocky Mountains cover a good deal more territory than Colorado. In the United States, the mountains stretch over ten states; from Idaho and Montana in the North to the southern reaches of New Mexico and Arizona. The extreme distances that separate those states have had a distinctive effect on social, economic and cultural development. A Coloradoan is as different from someone who has grown up in northern Wyoming as they both are from a native of southern Utah. But the Westerners have a lot of things in common, perhaps the most important of which is that they aren't at all like the natives of the East Coast.

To compare East and West in the United States is like trying to mix oil and water. And the more you try, the more you emphasize the differences. The main emphasis in the West is placed on youth and the freedom it lives for. James A. Michener described it as: "its wild joy in living, its vital experimentalism in the arts and its willingness to cultivate new industries and new ways of doing old jobs." The Eastern view of it all, fortunately, has changed somewhat since Daniel

Webster's day when he described the West as "a worthless area." There is a good reason for that. If Webster could see what has become of the West, he would collapse in surprise. It was a region of incomparable beauty then, but the beauty is only part of the story these days. If he considered "worth" to be related to natural resources, he'd surely retract the question posed in 1852: "What use could we ever hope to put these great deserts and these endless mountain ranges?"

Consider this, Daniel Webster:

A metal called molybdenum, which is used to harden steel, and is the very best metal for making rockets, is found in abundance in the Colorado Rockies – half the world's supply, in fact. Some 40 per cent of the coal deposits in the entire United States are under "these endless mountain ranges." Oil is down there, too, in the hardened clay they call shale. In terms of personal income, Mr. Webster, people who live in your native New Hampshire today earn an average of $10,073 per year. In Colorado, the average is $11,142.

But Daniel Webster could have been forgiven for all of that. What did he know about molybdenum or shale oil? How could he have known that Colorado would some day become a center for publishing and printing and the manufacture of electrical equipment? But if he had only lived six more years, he might have bought a wagon and headed west.

In the winter of 1858 word began to spread that the Russell brothers, a family of gold miners from Georgia, had struck it rich along Cherry Creek. By the following March, the parade had begun. The area was vaguely known in those days as "Pike's Peak Country," and the wagons following the Platte River across the plains carried huge signs that shouted, "Pike's Peak or Bust." Not one of them intended to "bust," of course. There was *gold* in "them thar hills." One of the people who told them so was no less a person than Horace Greeley, editor of the New York *Tribune*, who made an inspection trip of what he called "the Kansas gold fields" in the spring of 1859. He went to a camp named Central City, not far west of Denver, and was astounded to report, in the first "entry" of *The Rocky Mountain News*, that the population of 4000 (including five white women and seven Indian squaws) was composed of people who had been there less than a month and that at least 500 more were arriving every day. The newcomers, he said, were "... sleeping in tents or under pine boughs, cooking and eating in the open (on a diet of) pork, hot bread, beans and coffee." But he noted that "a meat shop has just been established, on whose altar are offered up the ill-fed and well-whipped oxen who are just in from a 50-day journey across the plains." In spite of all that, the best advice he could offer his readers back in New York was to "go West, young man."

Greeley gave an honest report of what he saw in the Colorado mountains and he did see a lot of gold. But he tempered his report with warnings that the hard winters could make the mining season short and that the rugged countryside would make getting at the gold a tough proposition. He was also careful to point out that gold mining was no game for amateurs. But that didn't stop the hordes of young men from heading west, a fact that made *The New York Times*, Greeley's arch-rival, wring its hands and point out that the power of the *Tribune's* printed words would surely cause nothing but suffering and break up happy homes, not to mention filling New York's poorhouses to the rafters.

There was no need for a poorhouse in Denver City in 1859. It had a hotel, though. It was a log cabin. It didn't have any beds, but if you had a blanket you could sleep on the floor. Horace Greeley called it "The Astor House," because its rates were the same as the hotel he knew so well on Fifth Avenue back in New York. It cost more to have a drink out here, 25 cents a shot for pure alcohol with flavoring added, but Greeley didn't indulge. In fact, the original intention of his western junket was to deliver temperance lectures.

Actually in those days there were two cities on the banks of Cherry Creek and rivalry between them was so strong that when *The Rocky Mountain News* began publication in 1859, it had its office built on pilings in the middle of the creek in an effort not to take sides or to lose valuable circulation. The city on the western bank was called Auraria and if Denver City had a hotel, it boasted a school; the first "on the frontier of civilization." It was started by a man named O.J. Goldrick who startled the prospectors in 1859 when he arrived in town wearing a silk hat, a frock coat and yellow kid gloves. He had two college degrees and papers to prove it. But he had no paper money. His net worth after the trip across the plains was just 50 cents. That's where the silk hat comes in. He passed it among the miners asking for donations for education and in a matter of minutes collected $250. A few weeks later he opened the doors of the Union School, which on that first day had an enrollment of 13. His neighbors considered it a lucky day anyway, and used his enterprise as a means of luring new settlers to their town. They met every wagon train and proudly announced: "We have a school!"

It was indeed something to be proud of, but the city across the creek was growing faster. By 1860, Denver had its first skyscraper, a commercial building three stories high. Between them, Auraria and Denver had eight hotels, but the best were conceded to be on the Denver side. The Aurarians tried hard to compete with their sister city across the creek, but it was a losing battle. Things came to a head when entrepreneurs slightly to the west began tub-thumping for a new city of the future, the little town of Golden, whose very name was a promoter's dream. Seeing the handwriting on the wall, the city fathers of Auraria agreed to a merger with Denver. The marriage was consumated on April 5, 1860 in an after-dark ceremony in the middle of the bridge between the two towns. The name they kept, of course, was Denver, but the Aurarians were allowed to keep a semblance of a separate identity by being called "Denver, West Division."

The name Auraria was removed forever from the map of Colorado that day, but its namesake is still home to some 300 souls in the Blue Ridge Mountains of Northern Georgia. The name Denver was given to the mining camp on the banks of Cherry Creek by a delegation of settlers from Kansas who agreed it would be a politically wise gesture to honor the Governor of the Kansas Territory, of which this was a part in those days. What they didn't know was that between the time they left Kansas and came up with a name for their settlement, James W. Denver had been replaced as Governor of the Territory.

There is still gold in those hills, but it isn't a major industry nor even a growth factor in Colorado. But every once in a while an adventurer shows up looking for lost caches of gold. There are legends all over the place and enough old-timers to keep them alive. Two of them are similar enough to make you wonder about all the rest.

The first involves a group of Spanish prospectors who showed up right after the turn of the 19th century and struck it very rich in the southeastern part of the state. One of them got even luckier. He married the daughter of an Araphaho chief. He had no sooner settled down to enjoy life with his princess than the Utes and the Araphahoes went to war. The chief recommended that his son-in-law and his friends ought to leave for the duration of the war, so they packed their gold onto the backs of burros and headed for the Southwest. They hadn't gone far when they spotted a Ute war party. It was obvious they'd be dead if they didn't get rid of the gold they were carrying so they buried the treasure... several dozen 50-pound bars... under a rock. Then, after marking the spot with an old shovel, they raced off as fast as their horses could carry them for the safety of New Spain.

Rather than go back to Colorado, they eventually sailed back to the Old Country and their gold stayed buried behind them. A dozen years later, the Spaniard with a wife in Colorado went back but discovered his bride was dead. She had left him a beautiful young daughter, though, and he dedicated the rest of his life to making her happy, never once mentioning his buried treasure until the day he died. The daughter didn't care much for gold and promptly forgot about it. Years later she casually mentioned it to her son who wasn't nearly as casual about the prospect of being a millionaire. The only problem was that by the time he found the right field full of boulders, he couldn't find the right rock because the shovel was long gone. He never did find it. Nor has anyone else.

Another story revolves around an 1880s prospector who wandered into Denver with a report of a hidden mine not far from Sangre de Cristo Pass. He said it was so carefully hidden that nobody would ever find it without following the careful instructions he had written in his will, which left the mine and its treasure to his sister. The key to the instructions was a pick he said he had imbedded into a tree root with its handle pointing to the mine's secret entrance. His sister couldn't find it. Nor could any of a dozen searching parties spurred on by the publicity her plight had generated. Someone had taken the pick. That was in 1884. The mine, with piles of gold dust just inside the entrance, hasn't been found since.

True stories? Who knows? And there are others. Some say

there are a dozen chests of Spanish gold at the bottom of the Purgatory River and an Aztec treasure at the bottom of "Bottomless Lake" in Mustang Canyon. There's a cave, they say, *somewhere* in Colorado that is filled with Spanish treasure. Explorers thought they had found that one back in the 1930s because someone spotted a cross carved in a rock that might point them in the right direction. But when they went back for more careful exploration, people with guns who used the rocks for target practice had blasted the cross away and had pitted enough other rocks to make identification impossible.

With or without the help of vandals, the mountains hold many secrets. Hundreds of millions of years ago the entire area was covered by enormous seas, which is one reason why parts of Colorado look very much like tidal flats to people who come from coastal regions. They once were. As the seas receded, they were replaced alternately by subtropical forests and deserts. At various times, the seas came back, each time leaving a different legacy. Some 500 million years ago, for instance, the ocean left behind a wasteland and underground forces pushing rocks to the surface gave us the beautiful multicolored rocks that make a trip to the Garden of The Gods in Colorado Springs so memorable. Constantly changing levels of the water stratified them with a wonderful shade of red accented by greens, grays and whites.

It all took so long that our understanding of time in terms of eons isn't adequate. At various times it was an area of lush dinosaur-infested forests and harsh land that supported no life at all. But it is generally agreed that the mountains as we know them today were formed at the end of what geologists call the Mesozoic Era, which occured, give or take a few thousand years, about 80 million years ago. At that time a combination of earthquakes and volcanic activity gradually pushed the mountains up from the plain. Underground rocks were hurled to the surface and granite was tilted upward to form awesome crags and peaks. Meanwhile, lava poured from every convenient opening and then cooled to form solid rock.

Once that excitement was over, Mother Nature began a refining process. Wind and water conspired to wear down the rough edges, to fill in gaps with left-over volcanic ash that covered the nearby prairie, and to carve out canyons and gorges. Glaciers came and went and contributed to the process, leaving behind moraines and deposits of loose rock.

The Rocky Mountain system is subdivided into a northern and a southern range, and is again divided by broken plateaux extending from the Wyoming basin to the Snake River Plain. North and west of Yellowstone National Park in Wyoming and Montana, the Northern Rockies extend all the way north to Alaska. The Southern Rockies are considered by many to be less spectacular because they don't have the same concentration of massive spires and there are no ridges on the upturned foothills.

The Southern Rockies are mainly a series of long ridges with upturned sediment layers on each side.

There is a north-south division to the Rockies, too. It is called the Continental Divide. Technically, the Divide marks the middle of the mountains and rivers and streams flowing down the western slope eventually find their way to the Pacific Ocean, and water on the other side flows east to eventually empty into the Atlantic. It isn't a straight line by any means. In Colorado, it crosses the Wyoming border at the top of the Park Range but soon cuts to the east along the Rabbit Ears Range. After running east for about 50 miles, it turns south again and cuts through Rocky Mountain National Park. Then it heads southwest where it passes the headwaters of the eastbound Arkansas River, the westbound Colorado River and the southbound Rio Grande. It finally crosses the San Juan Mountains on its way to New Mexico.

Although the Continental Divide runs along the most spectacular of mountains, some of Colorado's more dramatic summits, like Pikes Peak and Longs Peak, are not part of it.

But the Rockies are not all towering peaks and bottomless canyons. Everywhere, especially directly under the tallest of the mountains, there are natural parklands, farms and ranches nestled on plateaux and in deep valleys. While the mountains may have seemed like an unconquerable barrier to early settlers, they gradually planted themselves here anyway. The soil is rich in many places. The forests are abundant with fur-bearing animals. There is a wealth of minerals underground. For all those reasons, it was worth it to them to make their peace with nature.

Gradually they found ways around the high mountains and where there was no way they either enlarged existing passes or constructed new ones in the high mountains. In later years, they even dared to build railroads through them on passes at elevations ranging from 7,500 to 12,000 feet. Explorers and builders have found 500 passes to help avoid climbing up and over the Rockies. There are 136 of them in Colorado.

Though the majority of the first settlers came to get rich, even those who never came close to realizing their dreams never went home again. The climate was better here.

Back in the days when the Pilgrims were grumbling about the weather in Massachusetts, the Spaniards were at work with their unique ways of bringing civilization to the Indians in Colorado. The Indians had never seen anything like the conquistadores, but then, the Spaniards had never seen anything like the Rockies, where Indians had been living for 20,000 years. The Smithsonian Institution has uncovered arrowheads north of Denver that are at least that old, and spearheads have been found among the bones of a type of bison that became extinct more than 10,000 years ago.

But the modern Indians that the Spaniards found lived their lives in a way much different from their prehistoric ancestors. The modern era in the Red Man's terms began in about 800 AD when a race of farmers appeared in Southwestern Colorado. They weren't warlike, but their neighbors were and to defend themselves they built their homes in the walls of the canyons. These early apartment houses were high up out of harm's way and featured large rooms capable of holding enough food and water to withstand long sieges. Some of the best preserved remains of these pueblos are in Mesa Verde National Park where scientists estimate the culture flourished until the end of the 13th century when they were possibly starved out in a great drought that lasted 20 years. They left behind so many clues about themselves that anthropologists can say with certainty that they suffered from bad teeth and often had stomach troubles and that rheumatism was a constant complaint.

By the time White Man began making his presence known, Colorado was populated by seven different tribes of Utes, part of the Shoshone Nation, and in the plains by the Kiowa, Comanche, Araphaho and Cheyenne. Though the plains Indians were cousins in the Algonquin family, they didn't get along too well with each other and were constantly at war. Occasionally they dragged the Ute into their disputes, but with the mountains for an ally, they were virtually invincible.

The wars between the tribes were fairly constant anyway. The plains Indians were not the sort to give up. The result was that, although they were not warlike, the Ute were good fighters and that, they thought, was an asset when the White Man came.

In the years when Philadelphia was still a small town, the Colorado Utes and their Navajo neighbors in the southwest joined in a conspiracy to harass the Spanish and kept at it for 150 years. They settled their dispute with New Spain in 1858 and for the next ten years contented themselves with an occasional raid on ranchers and prospectors who were moving in on them.

The Government in Washington solved this particular "Indian problem" with one of its famous treaties in 1868. Under its terms, the Ute were moved into the southwestern part of the Territory. But five years later it was discovered that there were minerals under the Indian territory and the Government moved them again. Those considered hostile were transferred to a reservation in Utah, the meeker ones were given a reservation in the Southwestern corner in an area that nobody else wanted. Their descendants are still there.

In the meantime, the Comanche, who like the Utes were a Shoshone tribe, were forced out of their home in the Black Hills of South Dakota after a war with the Sioux. They moved into Southern Colorado, which they used as a base for raiding parties into New Mexico and Texas, where they enjoyed the enviable reputation of being the fiercest of all Indians. Other tribes steered a wide berth around them, even their cousins, the Utes.

Then a tribe even more bloodthirsty appeared on the scene,

the Kiowa. After battling with each other for several years, the Kiowa and Comanche finally forged an alliance and then extended the hand of friendship to the Cheyenne and Araphaho. All four Nations bonded themselves together in 1840 and for nearly 30 years defended their hunting grounds against the White Man's "Manifest Destiny."

Manifest Destiny was the White Man's way of justifying the great move to the West in spite of the fact there were people there already. It was the will of God, they said, and heaven protect anyone who got in the way.

In Washington there was another justification. President Thomas Jefferson had purchased the area in 1803 for four cents an acre. He bought it from Napoleon who claimed he owned it because French explorers had discovered it first.

Even Napoleon didn't know what was out there. He had once planned to attack the British in Canada from the Pacific Northwest but decided to sell the land instead. Jefferson knew he had made a good bargain but he wasn't sure how vast this new territory was and so, in his role as Commander in Chief, he ordered a troop of 16 soldiers to march out from St. Louis to find the source of both the Arkansas and Red Rivers. It was vital information to him because Napoleon had sold him all the territory west of the Mississippi River but the territory in the Southwest hadn't been his to sell. It was "owned" by Spain. Jefferson needed to fix the southern boundary of the area the French called "Louisiana."

The little band of soldiers was led by Captain Zebulon Montgomery Pike who had been born and raised in New Jersey but had earned a reputation on the plains as a tough Indian fighter. He had a good reputation as an explorer, too, having spent ten years exploring the Mississippi. They arrived in Colorado in the winter of 1806 lured by a mysterious blue cloud that turned out to be Pike's Peak. True to his instincts as an explorer, Captain Pike set out to climb the mountain but he hadn't gotten far when a blizzard struck and he was forced back. Claiming that no man would ever be able to climb that mountain, he moved on to the south looking for the Red River, which the Louisiana Purchase stipulated as the southern boundary of French territory.

What he found instead was the Rio Grande, a mistake that was driven home when he found himself surrounded by Spanish soldiers who hustled him off to Santa Fe. He never did find the Red River and the boundary wasn't established until 1861 when a treaty agreed it would be the Arkansas River on the south and the Continental Divide on the west.

Official Washington still wasn't sure what it had gotten for its money and in 1820, President James Monroe dispatched another group of soldiers to have a look around. This one was commanded by Major Stephen H. Long who didn't think anything good would ever come of the flat country at the edge of the mountains. The historian attached to the party, Dr. Edwin James, put another myth to rest by climbing to the top of Pike's Peak, even though Pike had said no one ever would.

Both Pike and Long confirmed what the Spanish and the Indians had been saying all along: that the Sangre de Cristo range is among the most beautiful of all the Rocky Mountains. The difference was that these people kept journals which became the basis for newspaper articles and books calculated to fire the imaginations of the folks back East.

It was part of the game. The territory wasn't even worth four cents an acre unless people could be encouraged to settle there. Governments don't control territory, they control people.

Knowledge of the high mountains had already been recorded and expanded by the Lewis and Clark expedition of 1804. Jefferson had sent Meriwether Lewis and William Clark to figure out if there was a convenient way to get to Oregon across those mountains. They went out by way of Montana but came back through Wyoming because they found the Indians in the north a bit too hostile for comfort. Their southern return route eventually became the Oregon Trail which made it convenient, in a manner of speaking, for settlers to go west. Their journals, too, provided a public relations tool to make the move seem attractive.

Word that civilized life was possible in the high mountains was heard in the south, too, in the territory known as New

Spain. After the boundaries of the Louisiana Purchase were settled, about two-thirds of present-day Colorado had become officially Spanish. The rest was called Louisiana. When Texas won its independence from Mexico in 1863, Western Colorado became part of the Lone Star State. But Mexico disagreed. After Texas was admitted to the Union, the United States and Mexico decided that war was the only way to settle the dispute. When the smoke cleared the U.S. had clear title to all of Colorado, but agreed to respect the rights of all Mexicans living there. Following the rule that the only valid territory is a colonized territory, the Mexican Government had anticipated the war by granting huge tracts of Colorado land to some of its citizens. In this way, the million acre Sangre de Cristo grant, became home to six families who, in 1851, founded the town of San Luis, the first permanent settlement in Colorado. Three years later another group founded Conejos, on the Continental Divide side of the San Luis Valley. They were the ancestors of the largest ethnic minority in Colorado today; the Chicanos. There are about 200,000 of them in the state today adding a very special touch to the human landscape. The Chicanos are actually a blend of two distinct groups; Indian and Spanish, and they cling to the traditions of both. They represent one of the reasons why Colorado's heritage is as colorful as it is.

As colorful as Colorado and her people are today, nothing anywhere quite compares to the people who once roamed the area in search of beaver skins. They called them "mountain men."

From the beginning of the 17th century until near the end of the 19th, no self-respecting gentleman in either Europe or the United States was considered worthy of the name if he didn't possess a beaver hat. Every lady had a fur shawl and both sexes favored fur trim on their coats. It was big business.

In the early days of American settlement, trappers cut corners by hiring Indians to bring back skins for them. But by the time the frontier moved to the Rockies, the big fur buyers had established a preference for white men to do their trapping. Indians were too unreliable, they said.

At first glance you might mistake one of these mountain men for an Indian. Long months in the sun turned their skin the color of leather and what the sun didn't accomplish, a combination of soot and bear grease did.

To say they never washed wouldn't be quite true. Beaver traps had to be set under water, after all. But scraggly hair was almost as much a mountain man's trademark as the fringed buckskin clothes he wore. His shoes were moccasins made of deer skin or buffalo hide and often, when times got tough, doubled as a meal.

Every mountain man carried a long butcher's knife in his belt along with a pair of pistols. He carried his ammunition, about a pound of lead balls, in a pouch around his neck and the powder to fire it in a horn over his shoulder. Other tools of his trade were in a pouch draped over the other shoulder and he carried a heavy rifle, usually about .60-caliber, in his hands. The guns were of a special type made in St. Louis and were capable of dropping a moving buffalo from as far away as 200 yards.

In addition to his tools, he carried extra powder and lead, adding about 125 pounds of extra weight. He packed a pipe and tobacco, a bit of flour, some coffee and some salt. The rest of his food he picked up along the way in the form of nuts and berries and any sort of animal or bird that might cross his path. He also had a half dozen or so traps, but once they were in place he didn't have to carry them around with him.

Trapping was a seasonal business. The first run of the year began in the fall when the animals were beginning to get their winter coats and continued into winter until the ice got too thick to get at the traps. The second season started when the ice began to break up and continued until summer weather made the quality of the fur less valuable.

In the winter months between the two seasons, a mountain man wouldn't come down from the hills, but would make camp in a sunny spot protected from the wind and out of sight of wandering Indians. He spent the time preparing his skins and possibly reading. Many carried Bibles, some even carried books of poetry. For many of them it wasn't a completely lonely life. Some bought Indian girls to spend the year with them, for companionship of course, and also to keep the camp ship-shape.

After the spring season was over and the skins were ready, trappers from all parts of the mountains came together at a pre-arranged spot for what was known as the annual rendezvous. They stayed there for a month before going back for more skins.

A trapper could easily collect $1500 for the skins he brought down from the mountains. The companies that bought them from him would generally collect twice that much back in St. Louis. But the companies had other ways of making money. It's one of the reasons why the rendezvous lasted a month.

The wagons that were sent out to collect the pelts weren't sent out empty. They were loaded with trade goods that trappers used to keep the Indians friendly, with whiskey that the trappers used to help them forget their troubles and with all the other gear from tobacco to gunpowder that every mountain man considered necessities. The merchandise was sold to them at prices hundreds of times over cost.

During the month of the rendezvous even the most frugal trapper would be parted with much of his new-found wealth. But the rendezvous was worth it. After eleven months alone in the wilderness, it was a great adventure just to have someone to talk to. And to drink with. There was gambling to be done, fights to be fought, women to be chased after. The lucky ones who had anything left over at the end of the month usually used what they had to negotiate with the Indians for a girl to take back into the mountains. The price could be as low as a quart of whiskey, which went for about $4 at a rendezvous, or as high as a dozen beaver pelts, which could bring as much as $50 from a fur trader. It all depended on how young or how pretty the girl might have been.

When a man rode off from a rendezvous he was probably already thinking about next year's event. But out there in the mountains there were rattlesnakes and bears, high cliffs and deep ponds, angry snowclouds and hostile men with guns. There were Indians, too, all conspiring against the trapper's chances of remaining alive for the next year's rendezvous.

But if the mortality rate was high, there were always other men anxious to take their place. Because no matter what else could be said about the life of a mountain man, not one of them ever died of boredom.

Somehow you're never quite alone in the Rocky Mountains. You're in the company of an eagle soaring overhead, a chipmunk scampering out of your path. You're in the company of your own soul which can communicate with you here as almost nowhere else in the world. Off in the distance, the roar of a waterfall lures you toward it. The sight of it stops your heart. Above you, snowcapped peaks take your breath away. Below you, a cultivated valley satisfies your sense of order. In between a field of wildflowers invites you to run through them, to absorb their scent, and revel in their colors. Off in the distance a silvery lake reflects it all in water so clean and clear you could spot a trout twenty feet down. A magnificent elk crosses up ahead, stops for a moment to give you a disdainful look and then moves on as if to say he doesn't care if you exist.

But you care. You're in Colorado where existence is something special. It's a place where you wish you could stay forever, living a life that would never end.

Dusted with snow, the towering peaks of the Mummy Range rise majestically over a barren valley near Deer Ridge Junction in Rocky Mountain National Park ***above.*** **At the park's eastern edge, surrounded by the rugged splendor of the Colorado countryside, stands the popular resort of Estes Park** ***facing page.***

Liquor

Sculpted by millions of years of ice and wind action, tne craggy tips of the Rocky Mountains dominate the Colorado landscape forming a sturdy backbone for this, the highest of the nation's states.

Edged with the vibrant greens and golds of fir and aspen trees, Bear Lake's gently rippled surface reflects the deep blue of a cloudless autumn sky *facing page. Above:* **basking in the brilliant sunlight of an Indian summer Colorado's famed Maroon Bells overlook the lapping waters of Maroon Lake.**

Trembling at the merest hint of an autumn breeze, the rich golden foliage of the delicate silver-barked aspen, in the Rocky Mountains *below* **and the San Juan Range** *left,* **floods the Colorado landscape with its vivid hues. Glass-like lakes ringed by the tall, protective evergreens** *bottom left* **are a feature of the magnificent countryside.** *Facing page:* **the subtle gradations of late summer's greenery blanket the rounded shapes of the hills around Ashcroft, near Aspen.**

Home for innumerable species of birds and animal life, Rocky Mountain National Park *right, far right and bottom right* is an impressive mixture of fish-filled lakes, breathtaking mountain scenery and deep wooded valleys. Its 410 square miles of natural beauty are a major tourist attraction throughout the year, offering facilities for the skier, climber, fisherman and horserider. *Below:* hardy conifers carpet the lower slopes of the Sneffels Range in southwestern Colorado. *Facing page:* dotted with countless mountain peaks, Gunnison National Forest lies at the western edge of the Rockies.

he "Mile High City" of Denver *above* is important, not for its altitude, but for its financial
nd transportation facilities. *Facing page:* Colorado's gold-domed Capitol building. *overleaf,*
ft the business district, and *overleaf, right* the Civic Center, all in Denver.

Typical of the 1860s character of Black Hawk is the ornate Lace House, with its carved gingerboard trimming *bottom* **and the white weatherboarded building** *below.* **The town's brightly painted Crook's Palace lays claim to the title – "Oldest Bar in Colorado." Historic Central City** *facing page,* **scene of frenetic activity during the height of the gold rush, is now a sleepy town of some 300 inhabitants.** *Bottom left:* **Boodle Mine near Central City.**

TELLER HOUSE
ARMORY HALL
A.O.U.W.
McLAUGHLIN'S
XXXX
COFFEE
1869 GILPIN COUNTY JAIL EXHIBIT
Johnson's
SMORGASBORD

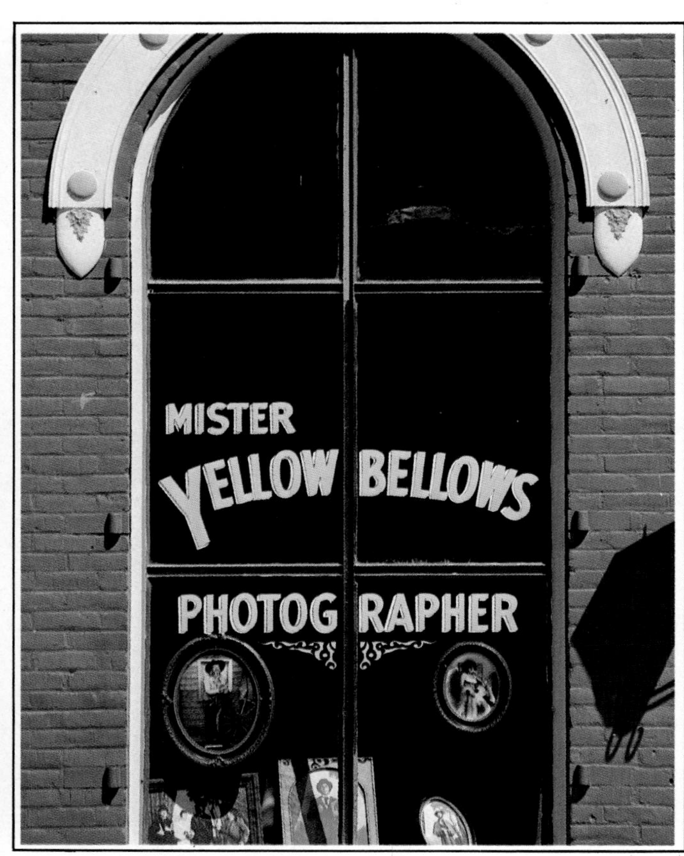

The colorful facades and bold signs of Central City's buildings ***this page*** **are a constant reminder of the town's recent past, when serving the needs of the prospector was as lucrative a business as prospecting itself.**

Delicate, yellow-leafed aspen and lofty evergreens appear to fight for space on the thickly wooded, precipitous slopes of Molas Divide Pass in the Rocky Mountains *above* **and on the hills around Ashcroft, near Aspen** *facing page.*

Ranging in color from cool, vivid green to rich copper-gold, the trees clothe and soften Colorado's rock-strewn hills, providing a stunning backdrop for the scene of cattle grazing near Doyleville in Gunnison County *right.* In parts almost untouched by the warming rays of the sun, the awesome Black Canyon of the Gunnison River *below* is deserving of its name. Majestic Monarch Pass, in San Isabel National Forest *bottom right,* at 11,312 feet, forms part of the Continental Divide between the Atlantic and Pacific Oceans. *Facing page:* nature's litter of sun-bleached tree trunks lies in the clear, shallow waters of Cottonwood Lake in San Isabel National Forest.

A dramatically setting sun over Interstate 10 seems to engulf the whole of the countryside near Las Cruces in its ball of flame *above. Facing page:* **the golden threads of lightning release the pent-up fury of a leaden sky during an electric storm over the Colorado landscape.**

The rushing waters of Crystal Creek wind their way through the splendor of the Gunnison National Forest landscape *above.* **Dazzling in their intensity, nature's vibrant colors blanket the land around Independence Pass** *facing page.*

Blessed with an abundance of fish-filled rivers, creeks and streams, Colorado's sparkling waterways, such as Tomichi Creek near Gunnison *facing page* and Quartz Creek near Parlin *left,* are a paradise for fishermen. Dappled sunlight and the earthy tones of fall's dying vegetation cast their magic spell on the Colorado woodland scene *overleaf* and warn of the more severe weather to come.

Caught by the light of the setting sun Red Mountain, in the San Juan range, shimmers in its incandescent mantle of gold *above. Facing page:* **the gurgling Cimarron River, rock-strewn and fringed with russet hues, weaves its way northward towards the spectacular Gunnison.**

The aptly named Crystal River *above,* **near the town of Marble, snakes through the thickly wooded splendors of Gunnison National Forest.** *Facing page:* **Tomichi Creek, seen from the heights of Monarch Pass in southwestern Colorado.**

Horses graze on the rolling plains of Gunnison County, near Doyleville *above,* **under the threat of a rain-charged sky.** *Facing page:* **the cathedral-like walls of the monumental Black Canyon echo to the sound of the Gunnison River.**

Crisp mountain air adds sharpness to the view of Shallow Creek Lake *facing page* which can be found eight thousand feet up in the Rockies, on a tributary of the Rio Grande. By contrast, the Blue Mesa Reservoir *above* is a man-made lake on the Gunnison River.

One of the many artificial reservoirs which have become a feature of the Colorado mountain scenery is the Blue Mesa Reservoir *these pages.* Set against the backdrop of the Rocky Mountains, the lake reflects that curious shade of blue which is only to be found at high altitudes.

It takes the Gunnison River over 150 miles to reach the Colorado at Grand Junction. Near its source the river passes the town of Doyleville and the land is good for grazing cattle and horses ***right.*** **Further downstream, near the town of Sapinero, the river has been dammed to create Blue Mesa Reservoir** ***below, far right and facing page.*** **Island Lake** ***below right***, **which reflects the peaks of Sheep and White Horse Mountains, also sheds its waters into the Colorado River.**

Pyramid Peak near Aspen *above,* **one of the town's many surrounding attractions, rises from a sea of autumn foliage.** *Facing page:* **McKee Pond near the town of Marble.**

Seen from a distance across the sprawling, scrub-covered San Luis Valley, even the mighty mountains appear intimidated by the oppressive, leaden sky *above.* Huddled together as if for protection, the forests of aspen *facing page* spread their warm colors over the land.

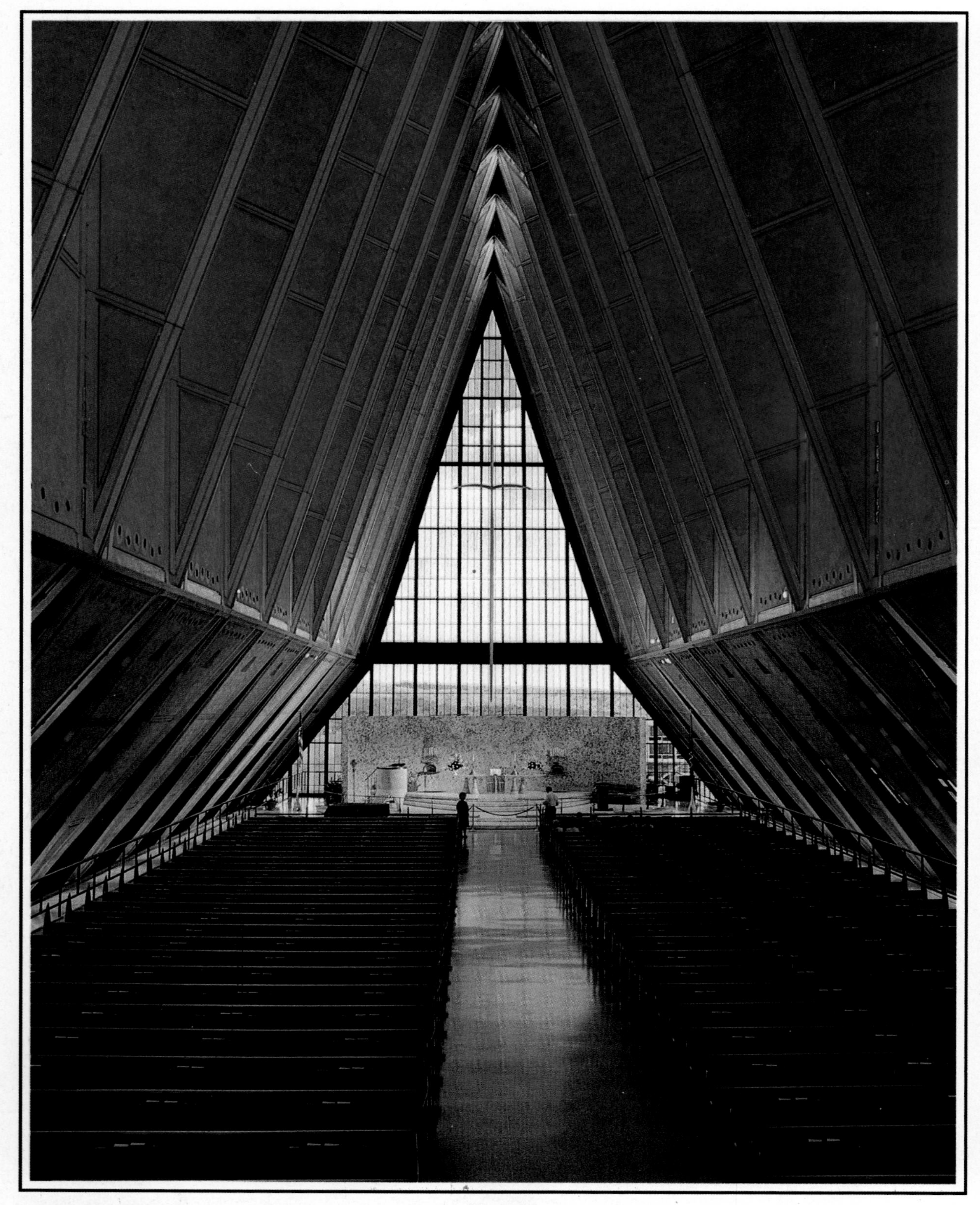

Resembling a futuristic sculpture, the glass, aluminium and steel Cadet Chapel at the Airforce Academy in Colorado Springs *these pages* soars 150 feet into the clear mountain air. The Protestant nave *above* is located on the building's upper level, with Catholic and Jewish chapels, as well as a meeting-room, beneath.

As if magically transported from some coastal location, the shifting shapes of the Great Sand Dunes National Monument extend for ten miles beneath the looming bulk of the Sangre de Cristo Range's western slopes *facing page.* **Equally unusual are the bright sandstone structures to be found in the Garden of the Gods near Colorado Springs** *above.*

The Shrine of the Sun *below left,* perched high on the slopes of Cheyenne Mountain, commemorates the famous humorist Will Rogers. *Left:* the Abbey School of the Order of St. Benedict in Canon City. *Below:* the restless 1000-foot high 'mountains' of the Great Sand Dunes Monument in the San Luis Valley. *Bottom right:* 370 acres of red sandstone rock, carved by the elements over thousands of years, make up the scenery of the Garden of the Gods. Mt. Sneffels *facing page,* its lower slopes thickly carpeted with a forest of conifers, soars to a height of 14,143 feet.

A cluster of wooden houses nestled high in the San Juan Mountains of southwestern Colorado make up the small community of Telluride. Originally a bustling town named for the element tellurium found in the ores of the region, Telluride's older buildings *below and left* serve as reminders of its colorful past. Today, the town is undergoing another boom with the development of skiing facilities. Silverton, with its preserved buildings *bottom left* and narrow gauge railway *bottom right*, was once the center of the San Juan mining industry. *Facing page:* the 'Sunshine City' of Colorado Springs, with the Broadmoor Hotel complex center left of picture.

Dubbed 'The Silver Queen of the Rockies,' Georgetown sprang into existence with the discovery of Colorado's first significant silver deposits. Many of the mines on the slopes of nearby hills are still visible from the town's main street. With some of its buildings dating back to the heady days of the boom period, Georgetown possesses a historic appeal that is reflected in such well preserved Victorian mansions as the Bowman-White House of 1893 *left* **and the ornate, boarded, Hotel de Paris of 1875** *below.* **Originally opened in 1884, the famous Georgetown Loop Railroad** *bottom left and facing page* **connects the towns of Georgetown and Silver Plume.**

The evocatively named town of Aspen, founded by prospectors in 1878, grew into a thriving community of 15,000 people with the discovery of silver. The crash in silver prices in the 1890s led to a decline in the city's fortunes and it was not until the 1930s that Aspen once again flourished – as a tourist and winter sports resort. Shown *below* is the Chapel of the Prince of Peace and *right* one of the town's brightly painted weatherboarded houses. *Facing page:* the frothy waters of nearby Maroon Creek. *Far right:* a woodland track near Dillon, to the north east of Aspen. *Bottom right:* the deserted cabins of Ashcroft; a ghost-town since 1900.

Tipped with leaves of vivid green and gold, the slender, gray-barked aspens weave colorful patterns over the Colorado landscape near Aspen *above,* **and languid Maroon Lake** *facing page.*

Seen from the gentle slopes of the surrounding hills, the town of Aspen *above* basks in the brilliant light of a late summer sun. Vail *facing page*, built in the style of an Alpine village, is well known for its fine skiing facilities as well as the attractions of the neighboring White River National Forest.

The textured timbers of a long-discarded wagon *facing page* echo the desolation of the town of Ashcroft *above*. The scattered remains of this once-busy mining township are now preserved by the Aspen Historical Society.

Perched precariously on a rocky outcrop by the Crystal River, the crumbling remains of Deadhorse Mill *facing page* **are a forceful reminder of the days when prospectors staked everything on their dreams of wealth. Crystal Creek** *above,* **Maroon Creek** *right* **and Granby Lake** *top right* **shimmer in the light of Colorado's cloudless skies.**

The rolling, green plains that front the mighty Sneffels range near Ridgeway *above* and Ouray *facing page* contrast with the rugged grandeur of the distant snow-capped peaks.

Seemingly carved for the purpose out of living rock, tne sheer sided jeep trails *above* enable the visitor to discover the hidden majesty of the Rocky Mountains. Imogen Pass Jeep Trail *facing page* unfolds a panoramic view of the sprawling Camp Bird Mine between Ouray and Telluride.

Mesa Verde National Park *these pages* **consists of a sandstone plateau which rises some 1,500 feet above the surrounding valleys. The park is renowned for its remarkable and seemingly inaccessible Indian cliff dwellings. The inhabitants, who relied on farming for their existence, were driven from the area in the 13th century by severe droughts. Much evidence of their skills and culture remains, however, thanks to the region's dry climate and the recent preservation work. The park is one of the Nation's major archeological treasures.**

Space Station
GAS

Thunderhead Restaurant, *above* **at the top of the scenic Stagecoach Gondola ride up Steamboat Mountain. Steamboat's vacationers** *facing page* **prepare to undertake the ski runs which radiate from the 9,100-foot-high summit of Thunderhead.**

HEAD

71504
11